Johannesburg
20 Must See Attractions

By Anton Swanepoel

www.antonswanepoelbooks.com

All pictures are property of

Anton Swanepoel

http://antonswanepoelbooks.com/
http://antonswanepoelbooks.com/blog/
http://www.facebook.com/AuthorAntonSwanepoel
https://twitter.com/Author_Anton

Introduction

Johannesburg, the City of Gold, has a rich history stretching back to the discovery of gold on the farm Lang Laagte. When George Harrison in February 1886 made the discovery, it set the stage for the gold capital of South Africa. When nine farms on 8 September 1886 were declared public digging areas, it sparked a mass influx of people to the area. All hoped to strike it large with gold mining. The digging area started from the farm Driefontein in the east to Roodepoort in the west. A town sprang up around the mining sites to support the miners, and Johannesburg was formed. At the time the area was only a settlement, and was named after two land surveying officials of the then Zuid-Afrikaansche Republiek (ZAR). The men were Christiaan Johannes Joubert and Johannes Rissik. The name Johannes they shared was used and 'burg' was added, forming Johannesburg. Some say burg means fortified city, but the Afrikaans name for the city is Johannesberg. Berg is the Afrikaans name for mountain. Thus it is Johannes Mountain.

Although there are numerous attractions in and around the city to see. This book focusses on historical as well as architectural important attractions. A number of additional attractions are included that will give visitors an African experience as close as possible to being in the bushveld, while being reasonably close to Johannesburg. A mixture of museums, parks and hiking attractions have been added to round the experience off.

Some of the important attractions include Constitution Hill that is the highest court in South Africa and an old prison where Mr Nelson Mandela was kept, Lilies leaf farm where Mr. Mandela once planned operations and hid from the government, a shopping centre with over 300 shops, a museum that houses the 2.1 million-year-old Mrs. Ples and other hominid fossils from the *Cradle of Humankind World Heritage Site*, the military and transport museum as well as Mandela and Tutu house.

Get 5 Important Facts You Should Know When Visiting South Africa + 5 International Travel Tips

Get The 10 Tips Here

http://www.antonswanepoelbooks.com/south_africa_5_facts.php

These 10 Tips can save you time, money, and make your trip go a lot smoother as well as help prevent lost luggage.

Table of Contents

Apartheid Museum

Address: Cnr Northern Parkway and Gold Reef Rd, Ormonde. Across the road from Gold Reef City and the Casino
GPS: 26°14'16.2"S 28°00'30.4"E
Phone: +27 (0)11-309-4700
Website*: www.apartheidmuseum.org*
Email: *info@apartheidmuseum.org*
Open: Tuesday to Sunday, 10am to 5pm
Entrance Adults: R85.00 | Children: R70.00
Best Time to Visit: Anytime
Time to Visit: 1 to 3 hours
Parking: Secure Parking in the Gold Reef City grounds
Guides: Guided tours are available. Contact +27(0)11-309-4700 (book two weeks to a month in advance. The author has no links to any guides used.)
Importance: Arguably the best visual experience you will get into the history of South Africa's apartheid years. If you have time to visit only one museum and wish to know more about the dark days of South Africa, then this is the museum to go to.

Anton Swanepoel

My Impression: From the moment you enter the museum, you are plunged into a new and shocking world. Even as a South Afrikaner myself, I was shocked to discover events that occurred and policies that were in place during my childhood that I did not know about. The museum has immense information to discover with a heavy focus on delivering this in a riveting audio and video format.

Opened in November 2001, the Apartheid Museum has become one of the top attractions in Johannesburg. Situated around 5km from Johannesburg centre and next to the Gold Reef City, the museum is often incorporated into a visit to the casino or the mine tours and theme park. Architects Mashabane Rose designed the museum to resemble the prison-like conditions of Robben Island while giving information on South Africa's apartheid years from 1948 to 1990, and later years with President Nelson Mandela leading radical change in the country.

The museum was built by the Gold Reef Casino as part of a bid to become socially responsible in the country's development. Initially the casino committed R80-million to the project, however the casino also committed to run the museum's upkeep for two years, which added around R20-million to their commitment.

The museum grounds occupies approximately 7 hectares and contains a natural recreated veld and indigenous bush habitat as well as a lake. A walkway takes you through the grounds and around the museum building.

From the moment you get your entry tickets, your world changes. Tickets consist of a plastic card that denote either 'white' or 'non-white'. Following this, you enter through a turnstile and down a steel mesh walkway that visually and physically lets you experience the apartheid years. After the stunning entrance, you are treated to a host of video and audio displays as well as images. Great effort has been made to source videos, newspaper articles, photos and objects from all over the world to create as rich as possible experience. The museum even includes a Casspir armored vehicle and 121 nooses that hang from the roof, which represent the political prisoners that were executed during the apartheid years. Also on display are weapons that were used by security forces to enforce apartheid, racially-tagged identity cards, street and building signs (such as whites only), identity books and the hated pass books which controlled the lives of many people. Without this passbook, they could not legally work in South Africa even if they were a national.

You will be forgiven for walking out of the museum with the feeling that you were in the townships dodging bullets and teargas canisters. Outside the museum, you can relax next to the small lake and have something to eat and drink at the onsite restaurant.

Special Note: The museum displays graphic images of brutality in both film, audio, and print and is therefore not appropriate for children under the age of 11 or sensitive people.

Carlton Centre

Address: Main entrance at 119 Main Street, Johannesburg
GPS: 26°12'22.4"S 28°02'48.9"E
Phone: +27(0)11-308-1331
Open: Open daily from 7am-10pm
Entrance Fee: R15 to ride to the top. (Not always open)
Best Time to Visit: Weekdays, in the morning
Parking: There is paid parking across the mall entrance at 140 Main Street (Small Street Parkade)
Time to Visit: 45 minutes to 2 hours (if shopping)
Importance: Tallest shopping building in Africa

My Impression: Although Carlton Centre remains a favorite attraction to tourists and locals alike, it is sadly starting to show its age and in some need of repair. You will find the usual brand shops in the Centre, however, if shopping is what you are after, you are better off going to The Mall of Africa that is covered later in this book, or Menlyn Park Shopping Centre, covered in my book *Pretoria: 20 Must See Attractions*. The main elevators did not work when I visited the centre and we had to use a service elevator and wait 30 minutes to go up. The restaurant and kuru shop on the top floor had been closed down, and some of the looking glasses (fixed binoculars) where broken. However, the top floor was clean, and although the windows were not spotless, they were clean enough to get some good pictures of Johannesburg. All in, even though the days of enjoying a meal in the tallest building in Africa is gone for now, the view over Johannesburg is still worth going up to the top.

Located in the heart of Johannesburg, the 50 floor, 223 meters (731.63 feet) Carlton Centre has been the **tallest building** in Africa from its construction in 1973 by Murray & Roberts. The only other structures taller than Carlton in South Africa is the Hillbrow tower at 270 meters (885.83 feet) that was constructed between June 1968 and April 1971, and the Sentech tower that is 240 meters (787.40 feet) high and was constructed in 1961. However, neither contain shops like the Carlton Centre as they are towers for transmitting and receiving radio, cell and tv signals. The closest building in Africa is the Ponte City Apartments at 173 m (568 ft) which is the tallest residential building in Africa. In late 2017, a restaurant called 501 opened in the Ponte building. At the time it was by reservation only. Contact *5101@dlalanje.org* for reservations.

Carlton Centre has over 180 shops in the lower level and 23 elevators to service the office floors. 6 elevators go to the top floor. Interestingly, over 46 percent of the floor area is below ground level. The foundations to hold the building up is 5 m (16 ft) in diameter and extend 15 m (49 ft) down to the bedrock that is 35 m (115 ft) below street level. The total floor area is 75,355 square meters (811,110 sq ft). The top floor is known as The Top of Africa. The building is currently owned by Transnet.

The Centre was linked to the 5 star Carlton hotel that was popular with the rich and famous. However, the hotel started losing clientele during the 1990s and in 1998 closed its doors after 25 years of operation. Some of the famous visitors to the hotel were Henry Kissinger, Francois Mitterand, Hilary Clinton, Margaret Thatcher, Whitney Houston and Mick Jagger.

From the top floor of the Centre you have a panoramic view of Johannesburg city, and is able to see the FNB Stadium (Soccer City) in the southwest, Gandhi Square in the west, the mining belt in the south, and Braamfontein and Hillbrow in the north.

Note that although you can visit the Centre by yourself, due to the high crime rate in the area it is advisable to visit it as part of a tour or group of people. If you go by yourself, use the parking across the street then enter by the entrance in Main Street. From the main building entrance, go down the stairs to the first shopping level and continue walking directly into the building. You will come to a small kiosk where tickets to the top is sold. The elevators to the top is on the right of you.

Constitution Hill

Address: 11 Kotze St, Johannesburg
GPS: 26°11'24.8"S 28°02'30.9"E
Phone: +27(0)11-381-3100
Website: *https://www.constitutionhill.org.za/*
Email: *info@constitutionhill.org.za*
Open: Open daily from 9am to 5pm
Entrance Fee: 1 hour tour R65 | Daily every hour from 9am to 4pm

2 hour tour R85 | Daily at 10am and 1pm

Night tour R300 | Last Thursday of every month with a minimum of 10 people needed to book

All tours are guided. See *admissions page* (*https://www.constitutionhill.org.za/pages/opening-hours-and-admission*) for more details. Tickets can be purchased on site or at *https://www.webticket.co.za/EventCategories.aspx?itemid=1465748877*

Best Time to Visit: Anytime
Time to Visit: At least 2 to 3 hours
Parking: Secure parking is provided at the hill
Importance: One of the prisons where former President Nelson Mandela as well as prominent apartheid figures such as Oliver Tambo, Mahatma Gandhi, Joe Slovo, Albertina Sisulu, Winnie Madikizela-Mandela and Fatima Meer were held in. Constitution Hill is home to the Constitutional Court, which is South Africa's highest court and custodian of the constitution.

Constitution Hill dates back to 1893 when construction started under orders from then President Paul Kruger. Finished in 1896, it was known as the Johannesburg Jail and mostly housed criminals from the rising mining town Johannesburg. After the failed Jameson Raid in 1896 where the British attempted to overthrow the Boer government, the Jail was retrofitted into a military fort. The conversion to a military fort was finished in 1899. In 1900 the fort was lost to the British forces who turned it into a prisoner-of-war camp.

When the war ended in 1902, the fort was employed again as a civilian jail. The old fort section only ever housed white prisoners, with the exception of former president Nelson Mandela. Mr. Mandela was housed in the old fort hospital section twice as he was deemed too dangerous to be housed with his people. The fear was that he may start an uprising or be able to run the ANC from jail. The first time Mr. Mandela stayed in the prison was in 1956, and the second time in 1962.

In 1902, two sections called Number Four and Number Five were added in order to house black prisoners.

In 1909 building on a section to house women prisoners was started. The section opened in 1910 and as with male prisoner, whites and other races were separated. Some of the more notable woman that were held here were Winnie Mandela (1958), Barbara Hogan, Fatima Meer, and Albertina Sisulu, as well as Daisy de Melker (1932). During the 1950s many woman were imprisoned for brewing beer illegally.

In 1928 a new section was added to house the large number of black prisoners that awaited trail. It was in the Awaiting Trial Block where in 1956, 156 people including Mr. Mandela awaited their fate in the Treason Trail. In 1958, 2000 woman including Winnie Madikizela-Mandela and Albertina Sisulu were held here for protesting the pass laws. Another influx of prisoners, many younger than 18 were held here during the 1976 student uprisings.

Conditions in the prison were harsh, with colored people suffering the worst. Blacks were often held for months while awaiting trial with no idea as to their fate. When a new black prisoners arrived, showering from one of the eight showers that served the thousands of prisoners were often forbidden for up to three months. Only after the gangs that ruled the prison allowed you in, were you given the right to shower once a week. However, even then you may never get a chance as the gang leaders hogged the showers. Thus, rain was always welcome at the jail. Except for the isolations cells (Emakhulukhuthu, the deep dark hole) that are situated at the end of the prison. The open air toilets' raw sewage ran past the eating tables down the prison compound and pooled in the isolations cells, especially when it rained hard. This sewage mix could often take days to drain away. In these cells were kept the dangerous criminals, those being punished for insubordination, as well as lunatics and those that carried infections diseases. The death rate in these cells were high and it was often seen as a death sentence to be placed in one of these cells.

On 31 January 1983, the prison from hell finally closed its doors. Inmates were transferred to the Diepkloof prison outside Soweto (South West of Town). The old fort prison was abandoned and slowly fell into disrepair.

In 1994, the precinct was renamed Constitution Hill and talks of building a constitutional court began. In 2002 its construction began. Except for a staircase, the Awaiting Trail Block was demolished and its bricks were used to build the court. Today the Flame of Democracy (lit in 2012 when South Africa celebrated the 15th anniversary of the signing of the constitution) stands in the left-over section of the Awaiting Trail Block to remind South Africa's of their right to a life free from oppression and injustice. The constitutional court was inaugurated on Human Rights Day, 21 March 2004. The Bill of Rights was recited in the country's 11 official languages by 27 children that were born in 1994, South Africa's first year of democracy.

The rest of the prison grounds were turned into a museum for tourists. An onsite open air restaurant offers light meals. Note that the Constitution court only gathers a few times a year, and is often packed as large trails appear in front of the court. The hearings are open to the public and media.

The old fort section can be viewed by yourself after purchasing an entry ticket. The Number Four and Five section is viewed with a guide, which is included in the entry fee price. Do look out for an inscription from Mr. Nelson Mandela's book "Long Walk to Freedom" on the roof of a passage to Number Four prison. The quote reads, "No one truly knows a nation until one has been inside its jails."

Ditsong National Museum of Military History

Address: 22 Erlswold Way, Randburg
GPS: 26°09'46.9"S 28°02'32.6"E
Phone: +27(0)10-001-3515
Website: *http://www.ditsong.org.za/*
Open: Daily 9am to 4:30pm (excluding Good Friday, Christmas Day and the first Sunday in September)
Entrance Fee: R40.00
Best Time to Visit: Anytime
Time to Visit: 2 to 4 hours
Parking: Secure parking on site
Importance: Largest military museum in Africa. Dedicated to all South Africans who have died in or as a result of military actions and a spiritual and symbolic home for all soldiers and veterans in South Africa.

My Impression: The museum has an impressive display of military vehicles and equipment on display. There is a rich history to be learned from the multiple display halls. I took my sister's kids (7 and 8 years) along and they had a blast. The war store is no longer at the war museum. See information on it elsewhere in the book.

The war museum is located directly adjacent to the Johannesburg zoo, and can be done in a day visit with the zoo. Up until the early 1940s, South Africa had no formal showcase to future generations of South Africa's involvement in WWI, nor of any local Boer wars. Capt J Agar-Hamilton who was appointed the official historian of the Union Defense Forces in 1940, helped with the formation of the Historical Research Committee that was tasked with the preservation of documents and military memorabilia. The foundation lay the drive for the establishment of a military museum.

On 29 August 1947, then Prime Minister of South Africa, Field Marshal J C Smuts, officially opened the war museum. At the time it was called the South African National War Museum. The following text is an extract from Prime Minister Smuts' speech. *We are gathered here today to open what may not unfairly be looked upon as a memorial to the greatest united effort our country has been called upon to produce. Memorials, of course, have more than one use. They serve to remind us of what is past, of great deeds of heroism and sacrifice; they also serve as a pointer, and sometimes as a warning to the future.*

It is in these senses that the South African War Museum may be regarded as a memorial. It will remind us, I hope, not only of the part we played in the recent great struggle to save civilization, but also of the horrors, the loss of life and the devastation, and serve as a warning to us to create a world in which we shall never have to use again the weapons of mass destruction we see here today, or those dreadful weapons to follow them.

The museum at first was to showcase South Africa's involvement in WWI, but WWII military vehicles and equipment were included into the display from the surplus after the war. In 1975 the Museum was renamed to the South African National Museum of Military History. It was decided to not only focus on the two world wars, but to include all military conflict in which South Africans played a part. Thus, military equipment and vehicles from different eras of South Africa's history found its way to the museum. In 2009 the museum was again renamed, to its current name, the Ditsong National Museum of Military History.

To date, the museum has over 44 000 items on display, which is divided into 37 separate categories. Some of the rare pieces on display are modern South African tanks, the Scout Experimental (S.E.) 5a and the Molch one-man submarine, and the real Mona Lisa. The Mona Lisa was the first jet engine fighter plane, which was manufactured by the Germans at the latter end of WWII. The plane on display was called the ME 262 and was the first line of two-seater night fighter planes. The one on display at the museum is the only existing plane of that make in the world.

The museum has a library on site that has a unique collection of books, journals and archival material that includes official South African World War II art and photographs. Note that the library is not a lending library and appointment has to be made to view the material on weekends.

Additional rare items on display are flintlock muskets from the 17th, 18th and 19th centuries as well as percussion-lock muskets and rifles. More modern rarities include automatic rifles such as the first models of the R1 and R4 assault rifles, and a German 7.92mm Fallschirmjägergewehr (FG) 42.

The memorial in the grounds of the museum was designed by Sir Edwin Lutyens, and was originally called the Rand Regiments Memorial and dedicated to British soldiers that lost their lives during the Second Boer War. On 30 November 1910, Prince Arthur, Duke of Connaught and Strathearn laid a commemorative stone at the memorial. On 10 October 1999 the memorial was rededicated to Include all people who died during the Second Boer War and was renamed the Boer War Memorial.

Note that the War Store is no longer located inside the Military Museum grounds and is covered separately later in this book.

Emmarentia Dam and Johannesburg Botanical Gardens

Address: Olifants Road, Emmarentia, Johannesburg
GPS: 26°09'10.5"S 28°00'12.2"E
Phone: +27(0)11-782-0517
Website*: http://www.jhbcityparks.com/index.php*
Open: Seven days a week. 6am to 6pm
Entrance Fee: Free
Best Time to Visit: Weekdays are less crowded
Time to Visit: 1 to 3 hours
Parking: Has safe parking on site
Importance: Johannesburg's main park and botanical garden. The park features a dam where you can row canoes on and catch fish. Dogs are allowed in certain parts of the park. Amazing walking and running paths. Bicycles are allowed. Has a small open air restaurant.

My Impression: This park is my favorite park to relax as well as to write. The food and coffee at the restaurant is good. The size of the park easily makes you forget about the day to day struggles and worries.

Located only six kilometers (3.7 miles) from the city centre, the park is a popular destination for picnics, romantic walks, cyclists, runners, canoeists, and dog walkers. With a combined area of over 81 hectares, the park easily absorbs the numerous visitors.

The grounds the park is on was originally part of a farm called Braamfontein that dates back to 1853. In 1886, Frans and Louw Geldenhuys bought a portion of the farm. Louw married Emmarentia in 1887. After the Boer War in 1902, there were a lot of Boers who had no land or work. Louw contracted many of the Boers to build a 7.5 hectares dam on the farm. He called it Emmarentia dam, after his wife. The wall for the dam was constructed from rocks that were brought down from the nearby Melville Koppies, and has a water depth of 20 meters (66 ft) at the centre of the dam.

Geldenhuys later donated the dam and an area of land to the west of it to the city of Johannesburg for the purpose of creating a park. The park was named Jan van Riebeeck Park in 1952, in celebration of the tri-centenary of Van Riebeeck's historic landing at the Cape. At the time, the park consisted of bare veld and no trees and was used as a sports field and golf driving range. On 19 November 1968, the director of the parks and recreation department submitted a report to the management committee of the Johannesburg city council for the creation of a botanical garden. In 1969, the approval was given for the creation of a Botanical Garden at the Jan Van Riebeeck Park, later to be renamed Johannesburg Botanical Garden.

Today, the park has a small restaurant that serves good food. Canoeing, sailing, and small boats are allowed on the dam (launched from the eastern embankment. Contact The Dabulamanzi Canoe Club, +27(0)11-486-0979.) Fishing is allowed on the shore near the public road. Dogs are allowed freely in the northern parts of the park. The park is a popular place for picnics, weddings, runners, cyclists, and nature lovers. The park itself houses a number of gardens, listed below.

The Shakespeare Garden
The Shakespeare Garden contains herbs that are referred to by Shakespeare in his plays, and include mint, chamomile, marjoram and lavender. A yearly Shakespeare festival is held in the garden to celebrate his birthday.

The Rose Garden
The Rose Garden is my favorite, and part of it can be seen in the picture provided. The garden has seven sloping terraces, with ponds and rose patches situated on each level. Japanese flowering cherries surround the garden.

The Herb Garden
In addition to ordinary herbs, The Herb Garden contains a section devoted to African medicinal herbs, as well as culinary and cosmetic herbs, in addition to herbs that yield oil and herbs that are used in the production of dyes.

Hedge Garden
The Hedge Garden has 58 different types of hedges, some that are trimmed, and some that are left to grow freely.

Arboretum
Californian Redwoods, English Oaks, Silver Birches and Cork Oaks from Spain and Portugal adorns the main arboretum.

Succulent Garden

The garden was opened in 2006 by City Parks MD Luther Williamson. Silica sand was used to create a dry river bed and gives the impression of a desert. Over 85 species of succulent plants adorn the garden, such as aloe, euphorbia, emblem, sansevieria and cactus.

Gold Reef City Casino Hotel and Theme Park

Address: 14 Northern Pkwy, Ormonde 99-Ir, Johannesburg South
GPS: 26°14'11.4"S 28°00'38.6"E
Phone: +27(0)11-248-5000
Website*: www.goldreefcity.co.za*
Email: *info@goldreefcity.co.za*
Open: Wednesday to Sunday: 9:30 am to 5pm. Closed on 24 December
Entrance Fee: Thrill Rider (ride all park rides) R210
Non Rider (walk though and eat at restaurants. No rides) R120
Heritage Tour R340. Mine tour only, add R100 to entrance fee.
Best Time to Visit: Anytime
Time to Visit: Minimum 4 hours to a day to make it worth while
Parking: Secure parking on site. Use the same entrance as the apartheid museum, across the road from the Casino

Importance: The best place to have fun for a day enjoying roller coasters and thrill rides. Apart from the Cullinan mines, the best place to get a tour of an underground mine near Johannesburg.

My Impression: If you like adrenalin, you will love the theme park with its heart stopping Anaconda and Tower of Terror rides. The places is a dream come true for kids. Locomotives on display show how gold was transferred in the old days. A mine tour underground is a must, followed by a show of how gold is melted and poured into bars. I sat in the front row and felt as if I could roast marshmallows from the heat coming from the oven. I was surprised by the science centre that mimics the Sci-Bono Discovery Centre in town. Sadly, the lower levels of the mine is now flooded, and the deepest pub in the world is no longer.

Gold Reef City Theme Park is situated across the Apartheid Museum, and down the road from the Gold Reef Casino, around 6 km from the heart of Johannesburg. The theme park is on the grounds of the old gold mine that used to be the farm Lang Laagte. When gold was discovered in 1886 in Johannesburg, miners flocked to the town. A spot on the 100km long gold reef that stretches from Boksburg in the east to Randfontein in the west was chosen for a mine. The mine opened in 1887 and operated for 84 years. The deepest depth of the mine is at 3.5 km. When the extraction process cost exceeded gold yield, the mine closed down in 1971. It is estimated that around 1400 tons of gold was extracted from the mine.

A reported 30 000 miners had worked over the years at the mine. With workers arriving from almost every continent, a way to overcome the language barrier had to be found. In 1910 a mining language called Fanagalo was invented. It took words from the around 50 different languages of the miners and created a language with around 2000 words exclusive for mine use. It is said that around 500 of the words are swear words.

In the 1980s it was decided to build a theme park on the grounds of the mine. The mine equipment and buildings were reused as museum and display centers. At first a museum was built at a depth of 215 meters (710 ft) but due to flooding the museum was moved to the 5th level at around 75 meters in 2013. A pub was installed and at the time was the deepest pub in the world.

Unfortunately due to the cost of having to pump out the water from the mine the museum and pub closed down after a few years and tours are now only allowed to go down to the 3rd level. The museum and pub are now on ground level.

A typical tour lasts around 45 minutes where you will descent down the famous shaft no 14 into the mine. A guide will show you around, leading you past a mine manager's station, a cocopan that takes 1 ton of rock, a dynamite box, a mock miner that drills into the wall, and other equipment. From one cocopan the mine typically yields around 4 grams of gold. Above ground again, you can see how gold-pouring is done, then walk around the Victorian styled houses and geological displays. There are a number of restaurant to eat at, as well as a cinema. For those that love adventure, the multitude of thrill rides offer from a 1 to a 10 on the fear factor scale. The wildest is the Tower of Terror at a fear factor of 10. Have a heart stopping experience as you plunge down 90-degrees from 50 meters (165ft) at a speed of 100 kph (62mph) into an open mine shaft. For the kids, there is an animal farm and a science centre.

Gold Reef Casino across the road has 1 700 slot machines and 50 gaming tables. It also has a spacious lounge area with an exclusive Salon Privé gaming lounge reserved for high rollers. There are places to dine inside as well.

James Hall Transport Museum

Address: Pioneers' Park, Rosettenville Road, La Rochelle (Entrance in Turf road)
GPS: 26°14'03.7"S 28°03'11.4"E
Phone: +27(0)11-435-9718 or +27(0)11-435-9485/6/7
Website: *http://www.jhmt.org.za/*
Open: Tuesday to Friday. 9am to midday, then 1pm to 4:30 pm. Thus closed for lunch from midday to 1pm.
Entrance Fee: Free. (Donations asked)
Best Time to Visit: Mornings are less crowded
Time to Visit: 1 to 2 hours
Parking: Has safe parking on site
Importance: The largest and most comprehensive museum of land transport in South Africa

My Impression: There is so much to see and learn in the museum. Not only about cars, buses and trains, but also the trams that were used in South Africa, as well as the history of tires. I liked being able to climb into some of the trams and locomotives.

Located a few kilometers from the city centre, the transport museum is a hidden gem. The museum was established in February 1964 by the late Jimmie Hall. The museum has seven display areas (5 halls, a courtyard and a porch). The museum displays the history of transport in South Africa for over 200 years and has one of the largest and most comprehensive collections of steam-driven vehicles in the world including motorcars with the oldest one on display being a 1900 Clement Panhard. In total, more than 2500 items are on display. For two wheeled lovers, there is a range of motorcycles and bicycles on display, with the oldest one being an 1869 Velocipede (the boneshaker). There is even the only intact remaining front engined, half cab bus in the world, which happens to be the largest one ever built as well. Other rare items include a rickshaw that was used in Johannesburg until 1967, the last electric double-decker tram that ran through parts of Johannesburg back in 1961, fire fighting vehicles like the 1913 Merryweather Steam pump and a 1959 Mayoral Rolls Royce, a 1957 Messerschmitt model KR200, and a 1959 B.M.W. Isetta model 300.

A short list of some of what are on offer:
Animal-drawn vehicles: 1870-1910
Bicycles and Motorcycles: 1786-1960
Buses, Trams, and Coaches: 1891-1960
Fire Engines and Equipment: 1877-1960
Motor Cars 1900-1980:
Steam-driven vehicles: From the Anglo Boer War to the 1930s
Trams and Trolley Buses: 1896-1986

Johannesburg Zoo

Address: Corner of Jan Smuts Avenue and Lower Park Drive in Parkview, Johannesburg
GPS: 26°09'56.9"S 28°02'02.8"E
Phone: +27(0)860-56-2874 (cellphone) or +27(0)11-375-5555
Website: *http://www.jhbcityparks.com/index.php/zoo*
    and *http://www.jhbzoo.org.za/*
Open: Daily. 8:30am to 5:30pm (last entry 4pm)
Entrance Fee: Adults: R80 | Children: R 50 | Parking: R10
Best Time to Visit: Weekdays
Time to Visit: 1 to 3 hours
Parking: Secure parking at the entrance
Importance: Main Zoo in Johannesburg. Houses rare white lions

My Impression: The zoo has a more compact feel than the Pretoria zoo and can easily be walked though in a few hours. The Amazon display with its snakes, spiders and a glass tunnel where fish swim around you are amazing. The white lions are something to behold as well as how close on can get to a rhino.

Johannesburg zoo was founded in 1904. The 55-hectare land the zoo is on belonged to the late Hermann Eckstein who donated it to the city for recreational use. As a mining speculator, Hermann Eckstein was heavily involved in the development of Johannesburg. The suburb now called Saxonwold was originally Sachsenwald. It is here that Eckstein had 3-million trees planted.

When the zoo originally opened, it had only a lion, a leopard, a giraffe, two sable antelope bulls, a baboon, a genet, a pair of rhesus monkeys, a pair of porcupines and a golden eagle. The first enclosure housed the lion and leopard. Development of the zoo was slow with a Bandstand added in 1910 to host the popular brass band music of the day. The stone elephant and rhino house was built between 1913 and 1915. In the same time, an Asian elephant and a Bactrian camel were acquired. Both were used for entertainment rides. In 1936 a hospital was added.

From the 1960s the zoo saw rapid expansion to compete with international standards and drew larger crowds to the zoo. To help fund the expansion a decision in 1961 was made to charge all visitors older than 16 years an entrance fee.

Today, the zoo has over 320 species of animals, with an estimated over 2000 animals. Some of those included are white lions, rhinos, elephants, hartbees, hyenas, leopards, and wild dogs. With prior arrangement, night tours can be done at the zoo.

KlipriverBerg Nature Reserve

Address: Peggy Vera Road, Kibler Park
GPS: 26°18'13.5"S 28°00'38.5"E
Phone: +27(0)11-943-1312/2691
Website: *http://klipriviersberg.org.za/*
Email: *Lulamile@llt.co.za*
Guides and bird walks: +27(0)84-804-4073
Open: Seven days a week. 6am to 6pm
Entrance Fee: Free
Best Time to Visit: Mornings during the week is less crowded
Time to Visit: At least 2 hours suggested to walk from the one gate to the other (4 to 8km depending on if you take side routes)
Parking: Secure parking on site
Importance: Largest nature reserve near Johannesburg. Excellent marked hiking trails with coffee shop at entrance

My Impression: This place is a hiker's paradise and my favorite get away place to relax in nature. You can easily spend a day here in nature and do over 20km of hiking, or just do a short hike and sit on one of the benches provided along the trails. With the size of the place and local wild life, you will be forgiven for thinking you are in the Kruger National Park.

KlipriverBerg (stone river mountain) Nature reserve is only 10 km from central Johannesburg and close to the highway. With around 700 ha to explore, it is the largest proclaimed nature reserve near Johannesburg. The reserve has from thick tree lines near the river, to grasslands and rocky areas when going over the mountains. All paths are clearly marked with colored stones along the paths.

Artifacts found here date to the stone-age and indicate that the area was used for hunting from the earliest of times. From remains of an abandoned Tswana villages with around 19 settlements it is clear that the Sotho speaking Tswana people lived and farmed in the area from 1400 to around 1750. Stone walls that protected the cattle are still visible. It is thought that King Mzilikazi eradicated the Tswana people from the area.

Sarel Marais was part of the Voortrekkers that came up from the Cape to settle in the then Transvaal. He and his family occupied the land in 1850. The remains of the farmhouse and graveyard are from the Marias family. During the Boer war in 1900, battles were fought in the hills. A concentration camp cemetery near the nature reserve testifies to the cruelty of war. The Marias family continued to occupy the land until 1950 when the Johannesburg City Council bought the land.

In the late 1970s, people requested that the land be set aside for a nature reserve. An agreement was reached, and in October 1981, the Mondeor Koppies Association was established to manage the reserve. The reserve was official opened in 1984 as Klipriviersberg Nature Reserve. The reserve currently has around 215 bird species, 650 species of indigenous plants and trees, zebra, black wildebeest, red hartebeest, porcupines, otters, blesbok, springbok, and duikers.

There are a number of marked trails from easy flat trails along the river to harder trails across the mountains with the longest trails being 5.8km to 9km. However, trails link up to each other in loops and it is possible to start on one trail and do a number of loops with linked trails and dramatically extent the original trail.

The remains of the old Marias family farmhouse and graveyard are still visible. It is thought that 19 family members are buried inside the graveyard and 57 farmworkers outside the graveyard.

There is a small coffee shop at the entrance that is open most days. Do bring plenty of drinking water with and proper hiking shoes as well as sun protection.

Lillies Leaf

Address: 7 George Avenue, Rivonia
GPS: 26°2'38"S 28°3'13"E
Phone: +27(0)11-803-7882/3/4
Website: *http://www.liliesleaf.co.za*
Email: *Events.co-ordinator@za.ab-inbev.com*
Open: Monday to Friday: 8:30am to 5pm. Saturday and Sunday: 9am to 4pm. Closed on 24, 25, and 26 December and 1 January
Entrance Fee: Adults R110 | Under 7 years Free
Best Time to Visit: Anytime
Time to Visit: Suggest a minimum of 2 to 4 hours. The main video is around 20 minutes then a quick walk around will take an hour without watching all the videos or listening to recordings placed in each exhibition
Parking: Secure parking on site

Importance: One of the best places to learn about the apartheid years and South Africa's struggle to democratic freedom. The farm where top ANC members were arrested before the Rivonia Trails. Once was the headquarters for Umkhonto we Sizwe (ANC military wing that is translated as 'the spear of the nation') and the liberation movement. Senior members such as Mr. Nelson Mandela, Govan Mbeki and Walter Sisulu stayed and planned operations here.

My Impression: This is a truly remarkable place. Even after visiting the apartheid museum and a number of other similar museum, Lilies Leaf still had much to offer. I was amazed at the multiple video and audio recordings around the place that gave a rich history into a dark period of South Africa. The house with its false drawers in the cabinets and the safari tour truck that smuggled arms through South Africa was a shocker to discover. The onsite restaurant has wonderful meals. Personally I found Lilies leaf more informative and less depressing than the Apartheids Museum as well as the Freedom Park.

Lilies Leaf is situated in the heart of Rivonia, outside of Johannesburg City central and 8 kilometers from the Sandton Gautrain station. For 18 months from 1961 to 1963 the events that were planned on the three acres property changed the future of South Africa drastically. The dramatic raid on 11 July 1963 that lead to the arrest of Lionel "Rusty" Bernstein, Denis Goldberg, Arthur Goldreich, Bob Hepple, Ahmed Kathrada, Govan Mbeki, Raymond Mhlaba and Walter Sisulu was thought by the then apartheid government to be a triumph. Yet, it was the start of the end of apartheid. The raid was the catalyst to more dramatic action towards change.

The Rivonia area consisted mostly of farmlands during the early 1960s. The Group Areas Act was still in effect and Rivonia was classed a whites only area, meaning that only whites could own land in the area. Arthur Goldreich was a member of the South African Communist Party at the time. Funded by a front company called Navian (Pty) Ltd, Arthur bought the land. Mr. Goldreich, his wife Hazel, and their two small children named Nicolas and Paul moved to the farm in December 1961. The outbuildings were already converted into hiding places for some of the most influential members of the African Communist Party. Mr. Nelson Mandela (nicknamed Black Pimpernel) had moved to the farm in late October 1961 already. Mr. Mandela took on the name David Motsamayi and acted as a gardener, cook and chauffeur for the Goldreich family. Mr. Mandela lived with the other servants in the servants' quarters. Many secret meetings were held at the farm. Other important members that found refuge at the farm included Govan Mbeki, Walter Sisulu, Ahmed Kathrada, Bram Fischer, Joe Slovo, Ruth First, Raymond Mhlaba, Lionel 'Rusty' Bernstein, Bob Hepple, Harold Wolpe, and Denis Goldberg.

The exact details of how the police got wind of the real purpose of the farm is unclear. Some say it was farm workers that told the police, while others say that George Mellis told his family about the cars he saw frequently entering the farm. Mellis was the son of the owner of the Rivonia Caravan Park, which was situated across the entrance leading to the farm. Reports and rumors reached the police, and an informant infiltrated the ANC party. The informant learned of the true identity and purpose of the farm.

Mr. Mandela was arrested before the raid on the farm. He was sentenced to five years in prison for inciting workers to strike and for leaving the country without a passport. On July 11, 1963, key members of the ANC party were holding a meeting at the farm. Although news had reached the party that the farm may be under surveillance, the party members decided to risk one last meeting before moving the meetings to Travellyn near Krugersdorp. In the meeting, Operation Comeback was discussed, which was a last resort strategy based on guerrilla warfare and government takeover that was successful in Cuba. With the meeting in full progress, police showed up in a laundry van. The police arrested 16 people that included prominent party members such as Lionel 'Rusty' Bernstein, Denis Goldberg, Arthur Goldreich, Bob Hepple, Ahmed Kathrada, Govan Mbeki, Raymond Mhlaba, Walter Sisulu, and farm workers who had no idea of the meetings. Mr. Goldreich was taken to the Marshall Square police station. Mr. Goldreich together with Abdulhay Jassat, Mosie Moolla and Harold Wolpe later managed to escape from Marshall Square. Mr. Goldreich disguised himself as a priest and fled the country successfully.

The day after the raid police discovered documents in a coal shed. The documents were in Mr. Mandela's handwriting and clearly detailed attack plans he was involved in as well as his diary of his African mission. This was positive proof that Mr. Mandela was linked to Lillies farm and attacks across South Africa. Mr. Mandela with others were charged with sabotage and terrorism in the famous Rivonia trail. Before the raid on the farm, Mr. Mandela had asked his lawyers to destroy these same papers while he was in prison. How different the outcome may have been had the lawyers followed his orders.

In 1989 Lilies Leaf was bought up by the Schneider family. Being unaware of the farm's history, they converted it in 1991 into a guest house and conference centre. When news reached the family of the historical importance of the place, it was agreed to restore the house and outbuildings, and turn the place into a museum.

In 2009, Lillies Leaf opened as a museum to preserve the importance of the farm, as well as showcase the struggle to apartheid. Today it is an important place for functions on the lawn, or in the on-site restaurant. The museum has a multitude of displays and is a treasure trove of information. The rare tourist safari truck that smuggled arms while transporting unsuspecting tourists is also on display.

Mall of Africa

Address: Lone Creek Cres & Magwa Crescent, Waterfall City, Midrand
GPS: 26°00'48.6"S 28°06'29.5"E
Phone: +27(0)10-596-1470
Website: *https://mallofafrica.co.za/*
Email*: communications@mallofafrica.co.za*
Open: Monday to Saturday: 9am to 8pm. Sundays and public holidays: 10am to 8pm
Entrance Fee: Your wallet
Best Time to Visit: During the week or early in the morning
Time to Visit: 1 to 3 hours
Parking: Secure paid parking
Importance: Largest mall ever built in a single phase in Africa and the largest mall near Johannesburg with over 300 shops

My Impression: I love the outside eating area with the fountain as it reminds me of Gateway shopping centre in Durban where I used to live. Although large, the mall is easy to navigate and boasts a number of upmarket shops that are not found in smaller shops in Johannesburg. One being my favorite to write at, Starbucks. The anchor shops such as Checkers and Woolworths carry items that are not always found in smaller chains stores.

The Mall of Africa is located in Midrand between Johannesburg and Pretoria, next to the N1 highway. With 131 000 square meters (1410072,26 square feet) of retails space and over 300 shops, the mall offers a shopping experience like no other. The mall was developed by Atterbury Property Group and took four years to construct. After a short delay, it opened its doors on 28 April 2016. From international brands such as Forever 21, Hamleys, Cotton On and Starbucks to local brands such as Checkers and Woolworths fill the mall.

The mall has both open air and closed restaurants that range from local favorites such as Wimpy and Spur to Mythos and Casa Bella. The large open walkways give the mall a light atmosphere. The mall is also one of only a few malls that boast a cinema with 2D, 3D, 4K, Cine Prestige, IMAX, and IMAX 3D theaters. Interestingly, the mall has the longest commercial curved LED screen in a mall in South Africa at 31 meters (102 ft) long and has the only ETFE roof (bubble roof) in SA.

The mall has a dedicated Gautrain bus route and stop. Pickup and drop-off for Gautrain buses is at entrance 5.

The design of the mall took inspiration from Africa's geological features. In the Northern Section of the mall is the Crystal Court that represents Southern Africa's mineral wealth with sharp geometric patterns. In the Eastern Section is the Great Lakes Court that represents the Great Lakes of East Africa and has a calm and gentle atmosphere. In the Southern Section is the Desert Court that represents the Sahara Desert of North Africa and uses traditional Berber carpets. In the Western Section is the Oleum Court that represents the West Africa's Oil wealth. The center of the shopping mall houses the Forest Walk Court that represents Central Africa and its rain forests.

If you want to enjoy a good meal or coffee with friends, fill up your wardrobe, or enjoy a movie, this is the mall to go to.

Mining District

Address: Main Street Johannesburg
GPS: 26°12'27.2"S 28°02'08.3"E
Open: Most restaurants are open from 9am, to 8pm
Entrance Fee: Free
Best Time to Visit: Early mornings
Time to Visit: 2 to 4 hours
Parking: A Parking lot is opposite Carlton Centre in 140 Main Street (Small Street Parkade). 26°12'22.4"S 28°02'48.9"E. It is a bit after Gandhi Square
Importance: Impressive open air museum of mining equipment as well as good dining. Has a replica of the golden rhino
My Impression: The architecture is amazing and seeing and reading about the struggle of Mr. Mandela to become a lawyer in the city was interesting

Main Street starts at the Johannesburg Central Court and runs through Main Street Square (Marshall Square) (26°12'26.3"S 28°02'16.7"E) and Gandhi Square. All in about 780 meters. It is suggested to start at Main Street Square if you do not have time to walk the entire road. All along the way you will find mining machinery, as well as open air café's. The open air museum is informative and portrays the history and legacy of mining in South Africa. The street is also home to some of the world's largest mining companies.

One of the best places to rest and have something to eat and drink is City Perk Café with its outdoor tables in Hollard Street. Do have a look at the Mapungubwe Golden Rhino a bit down the road from the City Perk Café. This statue is a representation of the golden rhinoceros that was retrieved in 1932 from a royal burial site at Mapungubwe Hill, situated north of the Limpopo River. The actual statue is in the Mapungubwe Museum at the University of Pretoria and dates back over 800 years to a time when an ancient black society lived at Mapungubwe. They traded gold with the East via the Mozambican coast. However, at the time of writing the museum was closed with no indication of when the museum will open again. If interested contact *http://www.up.ac.za/museums-collections.*

The Impala Stampede sculpture was donated by the Oppenheimer family in 1960. The Bear and Bull sculpture is a remnant of the street's stock exchange heyday. A historic stamp mill that was once used to crush rocks at one of Johannesburg's first mines is situated in front of the Chamber of Mines. A mine-shaft museum is at the Standard Bank head office in Simmonds Street. While in the Standard Bank building, visit the Standard Bank Art Gallery (not open on Sundays). Do have a look at Chancellor House in Fox Street, just around the corner from the Magistrate Court at the start of Main Street. 26°12'24.8"S 28°02'04.3"E. It has a sidewalk museum that tells the story of when Mr. Nelson Mandela and Mr. Oliver Tambo launched the country's first black law practice on this spot in the 1950s.

Mushroom Farm Park

Address: Daisy Street, off Rivonia Road (opposite Radisson Blu Hotel), Sandton Central, Johannesburg
GPS: 26°06'15.9"S 28°03'42.1"E
Phone: +27(0)11-784-6881
Website: *http://www.joburg.co.za/mushroom-farm-park/*
Open: Seven days a week. 6am to 6pm
Entrance Fee: Free
Best Time to Visit: Anytime
Time to Visit: 30 minutes to 2 hours
Importance: Lovely enclosed park in the heart of the city. Ideal for families with small kids
My Impression: The park was in very good condition when I visited it, with a number of families enjoying the facilities. I love the fact that it is a small park that is easy to walk or jog around in, while being enclosed. Sadly the air balloon was not operational at the time with no guarantee that it would reopen.

Mushroom Farm Park (renamed Hyundai Sky Park) is a small jewel tucked away in Sandton. The park is mostly visited by families on weekends. Although small, the park has a lot to offer.

From the parking area at the top, the park gently slopes downwards to a duck pond. The green grass is ideal for picnics, while a paved path runs close to the fence surrounding the park. You can walk or jog with ease around the edges of the park while enjoying the scenery. At the top of the park is a play area for kids. At the bottom of the park is an outdoor gym.

Security guards are situated at the top by the parking area. Toilets are available at the top by the parking area. Dogs are welcome, provided they are small (poodles and so on) and are kept on a leash. Be prepared to clean up after your dog however. There is a balloon in the park, which used to be operated by Hyundai. However, at the time of writing it was no longer running and there was no indication as to if the balloon rides would be made available again.

Origins Centre

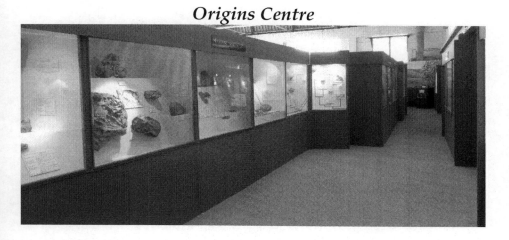

Address: Corner of Yale Rd and Enoch Sontonga Ave, Wits University campus, Braamfontein, Johannesburg
Phone: +27(0)11-717-4700
Time to Visit: 1 to 2 hours
Entrance Fee: R80
GPS: 26°11'33.5"S 28°01'43.4"E
Open: Tuesday to Thursday: 9am to 6pm; Friday: 9am to 8pm; Saturday and Sunday: 10am to 5pm
Website: *https://www.wits.ac.za/origins/*
Parking: Secure Parking on site. Go through the booms into the campus.
Importance: The museum displays the history of modern humans for the past 80,000 years, to its origins in Africa. On display is the hand and foot of Homo Naledi, our ancestor who was only discovered in 2013. The only museum in the world dedicated to exploring the history of modern humankind.

My Impression: I did the Cradle of Humankind near Krugersdorp first and found that the information in the Origins Centre adds great depth to the information given at the Humankind Centre. The history of the San people was fascinating to me, not only because I am South African. I highly recommend you visit the Cradle of Humankind as well, but if you cannot, then you will find great value and history of humankind's origins here.

The Origins Centre at the Wits University is often done as part of the Cradle Heritage of Humankind tour. The museum explores the history of modern humans for the past 80,000 years, to its origins in Africa. On exhibition is a large collection of rock art, ancient tools, and artifacts of spiritual significance to early humans. The museum focuses strongly on the early San culture and their rituals.

There is a café and gift store on site. Guides are available on site, or you can go unguided. The museum can be done by using the Red Bus service (*http://www.citysightseeing.co.za/*) (not linked to the author). The bus departs from the Gautrain Park Station and the Gold Reef City Casino hotel and stops at important attractions in Johannesburg. The museum focuses on the San people of Africa and the world's longest continues art tradition. The San people's DNA contains the earliest genetic print and links them to the Homo sapiens who lived 160 000 years ago. The museum also has a number of items on display about ancient fossils and the path of our ancestors to modern times. A basement and gallery level features 11 art pieces that illustrate the San people's history and give additional information on the San people, while an outside fossil exhibit has a number of plant and animal fossils on display, as well as the hand and foot found in the Cradle caves. Hand-held devices and video monitors at some displays give detailed information about the display.

There is also an example of a San gravesite. It was originally believed that the San people left their dead where they fell. However, evidence disproves the notion, showing they did care for their dead.

After viewing the museum itself, turn right just as you exit the museum (before going back to the ticket office). You will find a small fossil exhibition on the second floor. From the ground it does not look like much, but it is deceiving. A large number of fossils are on display, from ancient plants to animals, as well as Homo Sapien fossils. Right at the back, are various skulls of different human ancestors, as well as the hand and foot of Homo Naledi, our ancestor who was only discovered in 2013.

Right by the Homo Naledi foot, is a full skeleton of an Australopithecus sediba (the upright walking tree dweller ape). This is one of the most complete fossil human ancestors ever discovered. Another interesting fossil is that of a moment in time, 246 million years ago, a Lystrosaurus (plant eater) died by the river. While scavenging Lydekkerina amphibians started to eat it, the riverbank collapsed, freezing the moment in time.

SAB World of Beer

Address: 15 Helen Joseph Street (formerly President Street), Newtown
GPS: 26°12'15.5"S 28°02'00.9"E
Phone: +27(0)11-836-4900
Website: *http://www.worldofbeer.co.za/*
Email: *Events.co-ordinator@za.ab-inbev.com*
Open: Tuesday to Saturday: 10am to 6pm
Entrance Fee: Adults: R125 | Children under 18: R45
Best Time to Visit: Anytime
Time to Visit: 2 to 4 hours. Tours take around 1 ½ hours followed by a free drink (non-alcohol available) with the option to order a paid pub meal.
Parking: Secure parking on site or across the road at the Sci-Bono Discovery Centre

Importance: The place to discover the rich history of beer brewing in South Africa and around the world from ancient Mesopotamians to modern beer brewing.

My Impression: Even as a non-drinker, I found the place fascinating. The tours was well thought out and highly visual. An informative guide led the tour between multiple video displays and exhibitions. Definitely a must do if you love beer or are interested in how it is made and its history.

SAB World of Beer sits almost in the heart of Johannesburg. In the historic year of 1995 where South Africa defeated the All Blacks and won the World Rugby Cup, SAB decided to build a museum to commemorate the year. 1995 also marked South Africa's first full year as a democracy. The museum was one of many investments into the Newton district and paved the way for additional investment into Johannesburg.

Tours run on the hour and consists of a guided walk through the museum. A number of exhibitions with videos showcase the rich history of beer making from ancient Mesopotamians to modern beer brewing. There are actual mixers on display (one is pictured above) where one can see a simulated process of beer making.

Some of the old items used such as a delivery truck and desk of the founders of SAB are on display. A local pub and schebeen are also on display. After the tour you have the opportunity to enjoy a paid pub meal at the onsite pub as well as taste a wide variety of beers. At the time of writing a free beer or soda was included in the tour price.

Sci-Bono Discovery Centre

Address: Miriam Makeba St & Helen Joseph Street, Newtown
GPS: 26°12'15.2"S 28°02'00.2"E
Phone: +27(0)11-639-8400
Website*: http://www.sci-bono.co.za/*
Email: *info@sci-bono.co.za*
Open: Monday to Friday 9am to 5pm
         Saturday and Sunday 9am to 4:30pm
Entrance Fee: Adults: R48
          Children 3 to 16 years old: R32
          Children under 3 years old: Free
          Family ticket (2 adults and 2 children): R140
Best Time to Visit: Weekdays
Time to Visit: At least 2 to 4 hours
Parking: Secure Parking is provided in front of the centre

Importance: The best interactive science and technology education for kids in Gauteng and Southern Africa's largest science centre. Kids learn all about maths, science, and technology while having immense fun interacting with the teaching devices.

My Impression: I felt like a kid again playing with the different science and technology devices. It was amazing to be able to see inside a car's gearbox while I operate it by changing gears. I could see exactly how the gears are changed and selected. I had to laugh at the school kids that tried to outdo each other by cycling on a standing bicycle that runs a dynamo and powers up a sequence of lights the faster you cycle. This is a place to let kids play and expand their minds.

Situated across from SAB World of beer almost in the heart of Johannesburg, Sci-Bono Discovery Centre is a world-class science centre dedicated to the education of maths, science and technology through innovative visual and physical learning experiences. Being Southern Africa's largest science centre it should be on the top of attractions to visit for any parent with young children, as well as those young at heart that have a passion for learning.

The building was originally an old power station and was retrofitted with an immense array of science and technology displays. Geared towards children, the displays offer children various ways of discovering and learning science while having fun. From operating a crane that picks up sponge blocks to seeing how a motorcar's gearbox works internally to seeing refractions in crystals and cycling on a stationary bicycle to get a light bulb burning.

There are multiple levels that children can safely navigate, with the PlayStation games level one of the most popular. There is a small onside restaurant that offers coffee, tee and sandwiches.

South African Airways Museum

Address: Aviation Museum complex, Off Dakota Crescent, Rand Airport, Germiston
GPS: 26°14'30.5"S 28°09'33.6"E
Phone: +27(0)76-879-5044
Website*: http://www.saamuseum.co.za/*
E-mail*: info@saamuseum.co.za*
Open: Tuesday to Sunday: 9am to 3pm
Closed: 25 and 26 December, and 1 January
Entrance Fee: Adults R40 | Children R25
Best Time to Visit: Anytime
Time to Visit: 2 to 4 hours
Parking: Secure parking on site
Importance: The only Aviation Museum dedicated to the preservation of Civil Aviation in South Africa.

My Impression: What an amazing place with such a rich history of aviation and stunning aircraft on display. I loved walking through the old Boing aircraft and hearing the stories the airplanes had been involved in from the local tour guide. Inside the museum are an overload of visual aviation items.

The South African Airways Museum was founded in 1986 with the purpose of preserving the history of general civil aviation in South Africa with the focus being on the role South African Airways played. The museum was started with the purchase and restoration of the famous Junkers Ju 52/3m aircraft. The museum also has the world famous Boeing 747 (B747, ZS-SAN, Lebombo) that skimmed Ellis Park before the final World Cup Rugby match that South Africa won. The stunt was conceived by agency Sonnenberg Murphy Leo Burnett along with SA Airways and cost $40, 000 at the time. The same aircraft was also the official presidential aircraft for former president Nelson Mandela. The boing was flown to South Africa with a spare engine on the left wing as it was thought that shipping the spare engine to South Africa would take too long and be too costly at the time. The fifth engine however was not used during the flight and was removed upon landing and was thereafter never needed.

The museum has a collection of aircraft from piston to jet engine driven which includes a Boeing B747-200 and a Boing B747SP. Inside the museum display is an impressive collection of aviation artefacts and memorabilia that includes DVDs, books, toys, T-shirts, caps and more. There are also two flight simulators on display, one being a Boing 747 Classic. At the back of the museum is a pub and grill with good food and a wonderful atmosphere. A playground for kids is within eyesight of the tables.

Soweto Tour

Soweto (South Western Townships) is a township about 17 km south-west of Johannesburg, and is situated along the mining belt of the city of gold. When gold was discovered in February

1886 on the farm Langlaagte, thousands of people started to flock to the area. A then small town, Johannesburg exploded in size. By 1896, over 100 000 people had settled in the area. The south-eastern portion of the farm Braamfontein was settled by less fortunate white Dutch-speaking burghers (citizens) who had no land. Most of them made their living making bricks from the rich clay soul in the area. When non-white people started settling in the area, the then government unsuccessfully tried to keep the races separate. In 1901 and area called Kliptown that was part of Klipspruit farm was laid out for non-white settlement.

When in 1904 a bubonic plague scare ripped through the Braamfontein area, the government condemned it and burned it to the ground. Whites where moved to a different part of the farm Klipspruit than Kliptown. The area was later renamed Pimville, and then Newtown. Non-whites were moved from Braamfontein to Kliptown, which grew into the district now know as Soweto.

Soweto has many attractions, and is one of the favorite districts for foreigners to visit in Johannesburg. However, **never ever attempt to visit Soweto on your own**. Only go with a reputable tour company. Although Soweto is generally safe, especially in the tourists sections, it is too easy to take a wrong turn and end up in a dangerous section of Soweto.

As I have no affiliation with any tour operators, and cannot accept any responsibility for their actions, I will not recommend any myself. All I can note is that I used the Red Bus service for a tour to Soweto and found them at the time (2017) to be of exceptional service and well worth using them for the Soweto portion of visiting Johannesburg. Following is a short description of the normal attractions covered by most tour operators to Soweto.

Bara Taxi Rank

Bara (short for Baragwanath) Taxi Rank is the largest and busiest bus and taxi rank in Johannesburg. The taxi rank is situated opposite the Baragwanath Hospital and started out in the 1940s as a makeshift stop for the hospital. A visit to the taxi rank on a tour normally consists of a drive by. There are an estimated over 2000 individual taxies operating from the rank with a capacity of over 600 waiting areas for taxies. A taxi to any part of the country and some neighboring countries can be found here.

Chris Hani Baragwanath Hospital

The Chris Hani Baragwanath Hospital was built during the Second World War and is the third largest hospital in the world. The West China Hospital of West China Medical Center of Sichuan University and Chang Gung Memorial Hospital at Linkou are bigger. Originally named the Imperial Military Hospital, the hospital was built in 1942. It served as a hospital for British and Commonwealth soldiers. The hospital has approximately 3200 beds housed in 429 buildings. Around 6760 staff members are employed by the hospital. In 1948 the name was changed to Baragwanath Hospital. In 1997 the name was changed again to Chris Hani Baragwanath Hospital in honor of Chris Hani an ANC Party leader who was assassinated in 1993. Visits to the hospital on a tour normally consist of a drive by and at times a short stop near the gates.

Diepkloof

Diepkloof (Diepmeadow) is a diverse neighborhood and township in Soweto. The area was established in 1959 to accommodate the people that were being removed from the freehold townships of the Western Areas, such as Sophiatown, Martindale, Newclare and Alexandra at the time. The forced removal was due to a policy of slum clearance that involved the forced removal of Africans from designated areas. A visit to the area from most tours consists of a drive though on the way to other attractions.

FNB Stadium

FNB (First National Bank) stadium was previously known as Soccer City. It is the home stadium for the local soccer team Kaizer Chiefs and was built between 1986 and 1989. At the time it had a capacity of 80,000 spectators. In 1990, former President Nelson Mandela made his first speech here after being released from prison. Political activist Chris Hani's funeral service in 1993 was held here as well as a memorial service tribute in 2013 to Mr. Mandela. The stadium was upgraded for the 2010 FIFA World Cup and can currently hold 87 436 spectators (extra seating can be added to allow up to 94,736 spectators). The stadium is in the form of a calabash or Zulu clay pot, which is traditionally used for serving local beer (umqombothi). The stadium is the biggest stadium in Africa, and the 5th largest soccer stadium in the world when taking its maximum expanded seating. A visit to the stadium normally consists of a short stop outside the gates.

Hector Peterson Museum

The Hector Peterson museum is named after the 12-year-old boy who was the first person shot dead by police during the June 16 student protest in 1976. The museum was opened on 16 June 2002 and is about two blocks away from where Hector was shot. The museum also commemorates the around 566 people that died in the events that followed the day Hector was killed. The student protest focused on the sub-standard education of blacks in South Africa and the museum showcases their struggles during the years to fair education. Entrance to the museum is R30, and it operates Monday to Saturday from 10am to 5pm and 10am to 4pm on Sundays. Most tours allow you half an hour or so here or the option to take a second bus back.

Mandela House

Mandela house (Mandela Family Museum) is probably one of the most anticipated attraction on a trip to Soweto. The house is situated in Ngakane Str (Vilakazi Street) that in itself is an attraction with its open air restaurants. Mandela Museum is former president Nelson Mandela's first house he owned but not the house he grew up in. The house is a matchbox home and consists of four inter-leading rooms. Mr. Mandela moved into the house with his first wife Evelyn Ntoko Mase in 1946. In 1957 Evelyn moved out of the house following her divorce from Mr. Mandela. Following her marriage to Mr Mandela, Winnie Madikizela moved into the house in 1958. Although Mr. Mandela did not stay much in the house during his years on the run up to his arrest in 1962, Madikizela-Mandela and her two daughters Zeni and Zinzi occupied the house continuously. The house was petrol bombed and set alight several times during this time. In 1997, Madikizela-Mandela turned the house into the Mandela Family Museum and set up a pub and restaurant across the road.

The house currently contains an assortment of memorabilia, paintings and photographs of Mr. Mandela and is open daily from 9:30am to 5pm and costs R20 to enter.

Orlando Stadium

Orlando stadium is the first ever sports facility built for black South Africans in a residential area. It was commissioned in 1959 and has a seating capacity of 37139 spectators. The stadium mainly hosts soccer matches and is the home stadium of the Orlando Pirates soccer team. In 1975 Elijah 'Tap Tap' Makhathini defeated the world welterweight and middleweight champion Emile Griffith in a boxing match here. A visit to the attraction from tours normally consists of a drive by.

Orlando Towers

Orlando Towers are the remains of a decommissioned coal-fired power station. Now brightly painted with images, it is a stark difference to the smoke that used to billow from it. Construction started in 1939 and the power station was commission in 1942. The towers were added in 1951 to supplement the spray pond cooling system as it was running at full capacity. The power station operated for 56 years and was decommissioned in 1998. A suspension bridge is situated between the two towers. Plans to transform the power station into an entertainment and business centre started in 2006. However, on 25 June 2014, the power plant collapsed. One person was killed and five were trapped for hours. The collapse is thought to have been from theft of steel support beams. The towers featured in the movie Chappie and in an episode of the seventh season of The Amazing Race. Today, bungee and base jumping, as well as abseiling are done from the 100 meter (330ft) high suspension bridge between the two towers. See *http://www.orlandotowers.co.za/* for more information.

Tutu House

Desmond Tutu House is situated a short distance down the road from Mandela House in Vilakazi Street. No access is granted to the house. Archbishop Desmond Tutu with his family occupied the house from 1975 until the early 1990s. Mr. Tutu became the Bishop of Johannesburg in 1985. In 1986 he became the Archbishop of Cape Town, a position he served until 1996. Mr. Tutu was the first black man to hold each position. A blue plaque on the wall outside the house forms the main attraction for this stop.

Vilakazi Street

Vilakazi Street is the road that both Mandela House and Tutu House are situated in, as well as a number of restaurants, pubs and souvenir shops. Apart from the mentioned attractions, the road is also the only road in the world where two Nobel Prize winners have lived on, Mr. Nelson Mandela and Mr. Desmond Tutu.

Walter Sisulu Square

Walter Sisulu Square is situated in the heart of Kliptown, the oldest area of Soweto. On 26 June 1955, the Congress of the People met here to draw up the Freedom Charter. The carter is an alternative vision to the repressive policies of the then apartheid state. The Freedom Charter remains the cornerstone of the ANC (African National Congress) policy. It formed the foundation of South Africa's updated constitution in 1996. The square was named after Walter Max Ulyate Sisulu, who was a political activist during the apartheid era. The main attraction for the square is the open-air museum that explains how the Freedom Charter was written and showcases a round disc with the charter on it. See *http://www.waltersisulusquare.co.za/* for more information.

The Wilds

Address: Houghton Dr, Houghton Estate, Johannesburg
GPS: 26°10'27.7"S 28°03'07.2"E
Phone: +27(0)11-643-2313
Website: *http://www.jhbcityparks.com/index.php/list-of-parks-mainmenu-39/52-the-wilds*
Open: 8am to 5pm
Entrance Fee: Free
Best Time to Visit: Anytime
Time to Visit: 1 to 2 hours
Parking: Secure parking on site
Importance: One of the most beautiful public parks in Johannesburg. Dog walking is allowed provided that they are kept on leashes. Ideal for short and romantic hikes.

My Impression: This is a true hidden gem in the middle of the city. The park is dense forest in most places with easy to use paved paths. From the top by the Sun Dial one has an excellent view of Johannesburg.

Situated near the heart of Johannesburg on Houghton drive, the Wilds is a true wild place inside an affluent district. The land was originally owned by Barney Barnato's JCI Company and donated to the city in 1924. In 1938 the land was developed into a public park. It was decided to leave much of the park in a wild state and let nature grow on its own as much as possible. Being cut in two by Houghton drive, a pedestrian bridge to connect the two sections was added in 1965. Wally Schutte and Brian Watt designed the bridge. The main part of the park is on Parktown ridge behind Killarney. The smaller section is across the road and hugs the edge of the Houghton ridge. From the Sundial one has a good view of the surrounding area. From the opposite side on the highest point of Houghton ridge you will have a great view of Killarney, Rosebank and Sandton.

Originally there was a memorial plaque dedicated to General JC Smuts, who was an acknowledged botanist. However, the plaque has disappeared over time. There is a plant display-house, which has been declared a national monument, although at current it is not in use. In 1981 The Wilds was declared a national monument and in 2006 a conservation area.

During the 1990s the park became a crime hotspot with muggings and rape occurring. In 2005 guards and police patrols were put in place to safeguard hikers. The park is now totally fenced off with guards by the entrance gate. However, it is still not advised to walk the park alone in the week. On weekends the park sees more visitors that increases safety. The stone walkways going through the park was in good condition in 2018 on my visit with the park clean. The park is peaceful and within a short walk you feel one with nature. With the thick growth and stunning beauty of the place, it puts most other parks to shame. With its smaller size and easy to navigate paths it is the perfect place for a quick hike to get back in touch with nature.

The Zone and Rosebank Mall

Address: 177 Oxford Street, Rosebank, Johannesburg
GPS: 26°08'41.1"S 28°02'38.1"E
Phone: +27 (0)11-537-3800
Website*: http://www.thezoneatrosebank.co.za*
　　　　and *http://www.rosebankmall.co.za*
Email*: marketing@rosebankmall.co.za*
Open: *First Floor:*
　　Monday to Thursday: 9am - 7pm
　　Friday to Saturday: 9am - 9pm
　　Sunday and Public Holidays: 10am - 5pm
Ground Floor:
　　Monday to Thursday: 9am - 6pm
　　Friday to Saturday: 9am - 7pm
　　Sunday and Public Holidays: 10am - 5pm
Entrance Fee: Your wallet

Best Time to Visit: Weekdays
Time to Visit: 1 to 3 hours
Parking: Secure paid parking at the mall
Importance: A vibrant mall with upmarket fashion, food and entertainment. It is a perfect mall to compliment the nearby Rosebank Mall.
My Impression: The Zone has been a favorite mall for me in Johannesburg for years. I love the open air restaurants as well as the cosy and relaxed feel of the mall. Although the mall is not large, it has some nice shops. However, it is directly next to the Rosebank Mall should you want to shop until you drop after your relaxed meal at the Zone.

The Zone is situated in Rosebank, a suburb to the north of central Johannesburg. With four floors, the mall is know for its lively fashion and good food. The mall is situated directly next to the Rosebank Gautrain station in Oxford Road (north south line), with the North train station exit being at the bottom of the mall. If you walk up from the Gautrain station exit past the outside restaurants of The Zone, you will come to the entrance for the Rosebank mall on your right.

In total there are six separate buildings, namely The Zone, Regents Place, The Zone Phase 2, The Zone Boulevard, Cradock Square, and Rosebank Mall.

The Zone is said to be the fashion favorite of the six buildings by setting a relaxed multi culture atmosphere. It has some of the trendiest and hip stores in the country. A number of coffee shops and a Cinema Nouveau adds to the appeal of the mall.

In addition to the mentioned attractions for The Zone, Rosebank mall next door offers two markets to enhance your shopping experience. Those being the Rosebank Art & Craft Market (*http://www.artandcraftmarket.co.za/*) that is open daily and situated next to Europa as well as the Rosebank Sunday Market (*http://www.rosebanksundaymarket.co.za/*) that is open every Sunday from 9am to 4pm and is situated on the rooftop.

The Zone is also the home of The Red Bus tours, currently the only hop on hop off bus service for tourists in Johannesburg. (Not linked to the author).

War Store

Address: 18 Bolton Road, Parkwood. (Entrance in Blandford Rd)
GPS: 26°08'57.4"S 28°02'21.2"E
Phone: +27(0)11-268-6999
Website*: https://warstore.co.za/*
Email: *info@warstore.co.za*
Open: Monday to Saturday, 7am to 5pm
Entrance Fee: Free
Best Time to Visit: Anytime
Time to Visit: 1 to 2 hours (if having a meal)
Parking: Secure parking on site
Importance: The best military memorabilia outlet in South Africa. Provides props and information for local and international films relating to South African wars.

My Impression: I was taken aback by the sheer information on display about wars that South Africa were involved in. Having served in the South African defense force myself, I had a flashback of memories. If you are a collector of memorabilia from wars, or just want to know more about the history of South Africa, this is the store for you. There are also a number of books and films about WWI and WWII.

The Warstore is a unique experience for obtaining and selling war memorabilia or obtaining information relating to wars South African forces where a part of. The store used to be inside the Military Museum, but have now moved to its current location.

The store buys and sells anything from badges, uniforms, medals, equipment to other interesting items of combat. Items are sourced locally and internationally. The store even features on the South African version of Pawn Stars on The History Channel.

The store specializes in the following:
Angola war, Boer Wars (1890 to 1902), Border Wars (1960 to 1990), Korean War, Mercenary Actions, Modern RSA Militaria, Mozambique, Other African Countries, SA Police, SA Political, Rhodesia, RSA Homelands, South West Africa Wars, Zulu Wars 1880 to 1890, World Wars, WWI (1914 to 1918), Inter-War-Years, WWII (1939 to 1945). In addition are a number of Japanese full samurai armor and swords for sale.

The store has a nice on site restaurant that serves light meals at a good price.

Zoo Lake

Address: Corner of Lower Park Drive and Roscommon Road, Parktown
GPS: 26°09'36.0"S 28°01'42.5"E
Phone: +27(0)11-646 -1131 (8am-4pm)
Website for Restaurant*: http://www.moyo.co.za/moyo-zoo-lake/*
Email for Restaurant*: zoolake@moyo.com*
Phone for Restaurant: +27(0)11-646-0058 / +27(0)11-483-1017
Open: Seven days a week. 6am to 6pm
Entrance Fee: Free
Best Time to Visit: During the week and early mornings
Time to Visit: 1 to 2 hours
Parking: Prince of Wales Dr, Parkview, Randburg (26°09'24.3"S 28°01'45.6"E)
Importance: Main park near Johannesburg zoo and the venue for the annual Jazz on the Lake and Carols by Candlelight events as

well as the monthly venue for the Artists under the Sun open air art exhibition. One of the only parks you can row a boat on near Johannesburg.

My Impression: This is a wonderful park to walk around in, as well as have a meal afterwards. I love that you can row a boat on the lake and be so near to nature.

Zoo Lake is situated close to the Johannesburg zoo and is a favorite hangout for locals. Beit and Co donated the land in 1904 to the city. The land was divided into a public park and a zoological garden, with the park opening in 1908.

The park hosts important venues such as the annual Jazz on the Lake and Carols by Candlelight events as well as the monthly Artists under the Sun open air art exhibition. The park also boasts the Coronation Fountain, a Johannesburg heritage symbol, and the popular African themed Moyo restaurant.

The park has a number of open short green grass areas as well as thick tree covered areas. A paved walkway goes all around the lake and is ideal for jogging or a long hike. With plenty of picnicking, hiking and dog walking paths, one feels spoilt with the ability to take a leisurely boat ride on the lake. You can buy food to feed the local ducks, a favorite attraction for kids. An outside gym and a basketball court area tops off the list of attractions.

The restaurant is open daily from 8am to 10pm, with breakfast buffet served on Saturday and Sunday from 8:30am to 11am. Lunch buffet is served on Saturday and Sunday from 12am to 4pm.

Additional Attractions

Delta Park

Address: 77 Craighall Rd, Victory Park, Randburg
GPS: 26°07'39.2"S 28°00'34.1"E
Phone: +27(0)11-888-4831
Open: Daily from 6am to 6pm
Entrance Fee: Free
Best Time to Visit: Weekends are safer
Time to Visit: 1 to 3 hours.
Parking: Secure parking off road no 5
Importance: One of Johannesburg's biggest parks with bird-viewing hides. The Florence Bloom Bird Sanctuary is incorporated into the park. Dogs and bicycles are allowed. Ideal for bird lovers.
My Impression: The parks is large and have some beautiful nature walks from open grass to thick trees. A tennis court is included and a day with friends here would be well spend. However, with the park not fenced off as the Botanical Gardens and with no restaurants close by such as Zoo Lake, the park lags a bit if you are not a large group. Still, being less visited in the week a couple can have a very romantic walk here if they tire of the other parks.

Delta park is a 104 hectares grass and woodland park with ample walking trails that links three beautiful tree-lined dams. There is a playground for kids and a tennis court at the upper section near the Art Deco and restrooms. A number of bird-viewing hides are situated near the dams. The park is situated on the old Delta Sewerage Disposal Works that operated from 1934 to 1963. It was converted into a centre for environmental study and opened in 1978 by using the main buildings for the studies. The surrounding area around the buildings became a public park.

To walk around the edge of the park will take most of the morning. The southeast corner of the park is one of the most tranquil areas and perfect for picnics. Dogs are allowed in the park. Although recommended that dogs be kept on a leash, most are not. There are wheelchair access to most of the viewing areas at the dams.

The Florence Bloom Bird Sanctuary is an enclosed 7.5 hectare area and the oldest bird sanctuary in Johannesburg. Some of the birds that can be seen are guineafowl, various ducks, coots, moorhens, kingfishers, bishops, weavers, francolin, Willow Warblers, Great Reed-Warblers, Tawny-flanked Prinias, Sparrowhawks, Owls, Madagascar Cuckoos, Longtailed Pipits, and Ayres Hawk-Eagle.

Elephant and Monkey Sanctuary

Address: Road R104 Hartbeespoort dam, about 3km from the crossing with road R512 at the gas station after the dam wall towards Rustenburg
GPS: 26°12'15.5"S 28°02'00.9"E
Phone: Monkey sanctuary +27(0)12-258-9904/5/6/7/8
       Cell: +27(0)71-172-6965
       Elephant sanctuary +27(0)12-258-9904 / 9905 / 9906 / 9907
Website*: http://www.monkeysanctuary.co.za/*
       https://www.hartebeespoortdam.elephantsanctuary.co.za/
Email: *info@monkeysanctuary.co.za*
       reservations@elephantsanctuary.co.za
Open: Monkey sanctuary: Daily. Tours are on the hour, every hour from 9am to 4pm
Elephant sanctuary. Daily with interactions at 8am, 10 am and 2pm
Entrance Fee: Monkey sanctuary. Adults R315 | Children R180 (4 – 14 years)

Elephant interaction. From. Adults: R775.00 | Children: R335.00
(4-14 years)
Best Time to Visit: Anytime
Time to Visit: 2 hours
Parking: Secure parking on site
Importance: The bush babies sanctuary is one of several
sanctuaries that includes the next door elephant sanctuary that
provides for orphaned and abused animals. The Elephant
Sanctuary provides a temporary home for elephants and is the
only operation in South Africa of its kind. The elephant sanctuary
allows direct interactions with elephants.

The Monkey sanctuary is situated on 7ha of the Magaliesburg
Mountain alongside the Elephant sanctuary on the road leading
away from the dam wall towards Rustenburg. The sanctuary is a
new home for monkeys that were previously kept as pets. You
will experience a guided tour through natural indigenous forests
on elevated wooden walkways while seeing a variety of exotic
monkeys in a natural environment.

The Elephant sanctuary provides a sanctuary for mistreated
elephants as well as elephants that its owners cannot maintain
anymore. There are a number of programs ranging from viewing
to a full day program that entails brushing down an elephant as
well as walking with an elephant while holding its trunk. There
is also the opportunity to feed the elephants. An optional 10
minute elephant ride can be arranged per request on the day of
the ride if approved by the senior handler. The full day tour also
includes the monkey interactive tour. The Elephant Sanctuary
started in 1999 with five elephants and now has twelve.

The elephants at the sanctuary are Amarula (an old bull that used
to be in different zoo's in South Africa), Khumba (born 1990 and
the matriarch of the sanctuary), Mosadi (born 1990/1 and the

second in command matriarch), Temba (born in 2000 and the baby male of the herd and brother to Mvusu), and Mvusu (born in 1999 and is a playful young bull).

Hartbeespoort Aerial Cableway

Address: Plot 3, Melodie, Agricultural Holdings, Hartbeespoort
GPS: 25°43'16.7"S 27°53'04.6"E
Phone: +27(0)12-253-9910/1/2/3
Website: *http://www.hartiescableway.co.za/*
Email: *info@hartiescableway.co.za*
Open: Monday to Sunday: 9am to 4.30pm
Entrance Fee: Adults R195 | Children (4-14) R115 | Under 4 free
Best Time to Visit: Weekdays
Time to Visit: 2 to 4 hours
Parking: Secure parking on site
Importance: The best views of Hartbeespoort dam and the only cable car near Johannesburg.

Hartbeespoort Aerial Cableway is about 80km (around 1 hours' drive) from Johannesburg, by the Hartbeespoort Dam. From the top of the mountain one has a stunning view of the Hartbeespoort dam and panoramic views of the beautiful Magaliesberg Mountains. There is a small self-service express restaurant at the top and a Grillhouse and Pizzeria at the base station. There is a walkway with educational placards that describe points of interest seen from the top as well as a play area for kids. Paragliding is also done in the area. See *http://www.skywalksa.com/*

The cableway dates back to 1973 with the original cableway constructed using materials supplied by Swiss manufacturing company GMD Müller. In 2010, Zargodox (Pty) Ltd purchased the old cableway. In collaboration with Swiss company Rowema

AG, Zargodox upgraded the old cableway to new standards. The cars in use today are from Swiss company CWA Constructions, the largest cabin manufacturer in the world.

Johannesburg Planetarium

Address: Planetarium Building, Yale Rd, Johannesburg
GPS: 26°11'18.7"S 28°01'40.8"E
Phone: +27(0)11-717-1390
Website: *http://www.planetarium.co.za/*
Open: Shows are per schedule only, normally on Fridays and Saturdays. Confirm on website before going.
http://www.planetarium.co.za/publicshows.shtml
Entrance Fee: R35
Best Time to Visit: Be early for a show as tickets are limited to 400 people. *Tickets are sold from half an hour before the show starts and no entry is permitted after the start of the show.*
Time to Visit: 2 hours
Parking: Secure parking in front of building
Importance: The first full-sized planetarium in Africa and the only one in South Africa
My Impression: I took my sister's kids (age 8 and 9) to the show and they were fascinated by what they saw. When we drove away my sister pointed to the building and said that's where you were in. Her daughter's mouth dropped open and then she commented. "But I thought we were in a real space ship." That's how good the show was.

The Wits Planetarium began in 1956 when it was decided to purchase a Zeiss Planetarium for Johannesburg's 70th anniversary. Because of timing constraints, negotiations to buy the City Council of Hamburg's Planetarium was made. With the instruments in use since 1930, it had to be upgraded first to a Zeiss MkIII model in the Zeiss factory at Oberkochen. The city of Hamburg would at a later date acquire a new Planetarium.

The projector was then sold to the University of the Witwatersrand to be used to instruct students and the public about space and planets. The building to house the projector was started in 1959 and completed in 1960. On 12 October 1960 the first full-sized planetarium in Africa opened its doors to the public. The planetarium is also the second planetarium to open in the Southern Hemisphere. The planetarium ran constantly until the early 2000s. However, due to scarcity of presenters, the planetarium is now only operated on limited days and mostly only for kids using a prerecorded viewing. That said. The show for kids under 12 is a must do if you have the time when a show is being presented. The show starts with singing along and then time travel from the planetarium to the Kruger National Park, and then from there to space where a few planets are visited. All the while interesting facts are described about space in a language kids can understand.

Moddefontien Nature Reserve

Address: Arden Rd, Modderfontein, Lethabong
GPS: 26°04'52.2"S 28°08'19.4"E
Phone: +27(0)11-836-4900
Website: *https://www.modderfonteinreserve.co.za/index.php*
Email: *info@modderfonteinreserve.co.za*
Open: Tuesday to Saturday: 6am to 6pm
Entrance Fee: Adults non-rider R30 and R40 for a rider| Child R15
Best Time to Visit: Anytime

Time to Visit: 2 to 4 hours

Parking: Secure parking at the dam and at the restaurant. The restaurant is at the start of all the trail routes.

Importance: An easy accessible yet often overlooked piece of cross-country bliss that is only minutes from Sandton and Johannesburg International Airport. 24 hour security protected reserve that allows hiking and mounting bike riding, including night rides. No pets allowed though.

My Impression: I was amazed by the beauty of this hidden gem where one could walk and cycle in nature so close to my home and The Greenstone Shopping Centre.

Moddefontein Nature Reserve is a 275ha reserve just off the N3 highway, almost across from the Greenstone Shopping Centre. During the 1890s the need for housing for the growing gold mining industry resulted in the planning of a village in the area. In 1894 Modderfontein village was established. Most of the people living in the area was involved in the manufacture and selling of dynamite. This resulted in the Modderfontein Dynamite Factory being built that is still operational to this day.

A need for a reserve was identified and a piece of land was set aside for this purpose. The reserve was developed around four dams, named Fish Eagle Dam, John Voelker Dam, Grebe dam and Blue Crane Dam. Some of the reserve was allowed to grow wild, while other areas were developed to allow for picnics and braais with cut lawn. Hiking and cycle routes were set throughout the reserve with easy to read markings. The routes are especially suited for beginner mountain bike riders and hikers as well as kids. There reserve has more than 250 bird species which includes the African fish eagle and blue crane, as well as a small range of game such as steenbok and black-backed jackals with otters hiding around by the dams.

There are four main routes. The shortest one being the Orange route at 10 km that mainly follows dirt roads. The Green route is 18 km and uses some of the Orange route but then ventures into the bush. The Yellow route is 32 km and the Red route is 42 km. The red and yellow routes venture even deeper into the bush and require more skill and fitness to complete. Night rides are done. Normally on Wednesday from 6pm to 10pm. Do check ahead of time.

Due to the reserve being fenced off and access controlled, the reserve is very safe. There is a restaurant in the reserve, called Valbonne (*http://www.valbonne.co.za/*). The kitchen is open Tuesdays to Fridays from 8am to 5pm and 7am to 5pm on weekends and public holidays.

Suikerbos Nature Reserve

Address: About 14 km past the Sybrand Van Niekerk Highway crossing, on the R550 towards Diepkloof, Heidelberg
GPS: 26°27'06.9"S 28°13'12.9"E
Phone: +27(0)11-439-6300 / +27(0)79-439-0532
Open: 7am to 6pm
Entrance Fee: R22 per person plus R11 per vehicle
Best Time to Visit: Anytime
Time to Visit: 2 to 4 hours. The drive through is around 1 ½ hours if you do not stop to visit the museum and farm house.
Parking: Secure parking at the museum and information centre.
Importance: Being 45 minutes' drive from Johannesburg, it is the closest thing to Kruger National Park where you can drive a vehicle and admire the South African nature. Hiking and mountain biking are allowed.

My Impression: The drive out to the reserve was interesting in itself. The reserve changed from grasslands to rock hills to bush and gave one a lot to take in, in a short time. For the more adventures you can hike the reserve and be totally by yourself. The old farm house museum was a pleasant addition. You can bring food and braai at the picnic place about midway on the route through the reserve.

Suikerbosrand Nature Reserve is an 11 595-hectare reserve about 55km or around 45 minutes from Johannesburg, and is a popular hiking and cycling destination. With over 200 bird species, it is a bird watcher's paradise. Named after the abundant suikerbos (sugarbush), the reserve includes zebra, black wildebeest, red hartebeest mountain reedbuck, common duiker, steenbok, grey duiker, baboon, oribi, blesbok, springbok and kudu. Trees to be found include white stinkwood (Celtis africana), highveld cabbage tree (Cussonia paniculata), ouhout (Leucosidea sericea), sweet thorn (Acacia karroo), and guarrie (Euclea undulata).

The vehicle route is about 60km long, and will take you through open grassland, wooded gorge, acacia woodland, marshland and rare Bankenveld grassland. There is a wheelchair path (Toktokkie trail, 700m long) near the information centre that is close by the farmhouse museum and toilets. A number of hiking routes criss cross the reserve. The shortest is the Cheetah Trail at 3.7km with Bokmakierie trail being 11.5km. There is a caravan park in the reserve for those wanting to stay longer. The reserve does have self-catering chalets that can be booked from the numbers provided. The overnight trail are self-guided and pass six self-catering huts with a length of around 66km.

Two systems of geology are found in the region. The Ventersdorp and the Witwatersrand system consists of igneous rock that is called basalt and formed millions of years ago from molten rock. The Witwatersrand system comprise mainly of sedimentary sandstone deposited in horizontal layers.

Wits University Zoology Museum

Address: Jan Smuts Avenue, opposite the Biophy Library, Oppenheimer Life Sciences Building, Lower Ground Floor, Room LG 18, Braamfontein
GPS: 26°11'29.9"S 28°01'58.1"E
Phone: +27(0)11-717-6464
Website: *https://www.wits.ac.za*
Open: Weekdays: 8.30 am to 4.00 pm
Entrance Fee: Free
Parking: Parking is in the campus grounds, or in the road
Best Time to Visit: Anytime
Time to Visit: 1 to 2 hours
Importance: The Wits Life Sciences Museum is the only natural history museum in Johannesburg.

The Wits Life Sciences Museum is in the heart of Johannesburg, close to the Origins Centre and contains over 60 000 Zoology specimens and around 100 000 Botanical specimens. The museum was formed in 2003 when the Zoology Museum and the C.E. Moss Herbarium combined. The Zoology Museum itself dates to 1922 when Professor Fantham initiated it to help teach students. Over the years, Professors Van der Horst and then Balinsky oversaw the collection of over 40 000 embryological histology slides. To date it is the largest of its kind in the southern hemisphere.

The C.E. Moss Herbarium is named after Professor Charles Edward Moss who was the first professor of botany at the University. The herbarium was started in 1917 when Prof. Moss and Rev. F.A. Rogers went on collecting trips to Mpumalanga. At the time Moss was professor of Botany at the South African School of mines and Technology which was housed in a corrugated iron complex on Plein Square. In 1922 the School of Mines became the University of the Witwatersrand. In 1923 the Department of Botany moved to the Biology building.

The main display that is open to the public has skeletons, models and preserved specimens as well as tanks with live fish and other animals. The herbarium is open by appointment only.

About the Author

As a Technical Diving Instructor and Cave Diver with over seven years' experience working in different places, including the Cayman Islands, I have come to believe that limits are what you set for yourself. I used to be afraid of water until I forced myself into a diving course, and then things just kept going and the thing I feared gave me what I dreamed of doing, travel. Having dived to over 400ft on open circuit, I realize how much of life we miss if we let fear run our life.

Sometimes, life is like a dark tunnel that feels like it is going to squeeze the life from you. However, if you just keep going, you are bound to come out the other side. I love writing, travel, diving, caves, motorcycles, and speed, but as a Reiki Master Teacher, I know you have to balance your life with love, and compassion. Be proud to stand firm in your quest for your dreams, but humble enough to ask for help in reaching them.

More Books by Anton

www.antonswanepoelbooks.com

Novels
Laura and The Jaguar Prophecy (Laura Book 1)
Laura and The God Code (Laura Book 2)
Untamed Love (Aurora Book 1)
The Path To True Love (Aurora Book 2)

Travel Diary
Almost Somewhere

Peru Travel
Machu Picchu: The Ultimate Guide to Machu Picchu

Travel Tips
Angkor Wat & Cambodia
100 International Travel Tips
Backpacking SouthEast Asia

Motorbike Travel
Motorcycle: A Guide Book To Long Distance And Adventure Riding
Motorbiking Cambodia & Vietnam

Cambodia Travel
Cambodia: 50 Facts You Should Know When Visiting Cambodia
Angkor Wat: 20 Must See Temples
Angkor Wat Temples
Angkor Wat Archaeological Park
Battambang: 20 Must See Attractions
Bokor National Park
Kampot, Kep and Sihanoukville
Kampot: 20 Must See Attractions
Koh Ker Temple Site
Kulen Mountain & Kbal Spean
Phnom Penh: 20 Must See Attractions
Preah Vihear Temple

Siem Reap: 20 Must See Attractions
Sihanoukville: 20 must See Attractions
Shopping In Siem Reap
Kep: 10 Must See Attractions

South African Travel
South Africa: 50 Facts You Should Know When Visiting South Africa
Pretoria: 20 Must See Attractions
Johannesburg: 20 Must See Attractions
The Voortekker Monument Heritage Site
The Union Buildings
Freedom Park
The Cradle of Humankind Heritage Site

Vietnam Travel
Ha Long Bay
Phong Nha Caves
Saigon to Hanoi
The Perfumed Pagoda
Vietnam: 50 Facts You Should Know When Visiting Vietnam
Vietnam Caves

Thailand
Thailand: 50 Facts You Should Know When Visiting Thailand
Bangkok: 20 Must See Attractions
Ayutthaya: 20 Must See Attractions
The Great Buddha

Laos
Vientiane: 20 Must See Attractions

Diving Books
Deep and Safety Stops, and Gradient Factors
Dive Computers
Diving Below 130 Feet
Gas Blender Program
Open Water
The Art of Gas Blending

Writing Guide Books
How To Format and Publish a Book
Supercharge Your Book Description (Grab Attention and Enhance Sales)

Self Help Books
Ear Pain
Sea and Motion Sickness

Get 5 Important Facts You Should Know When Visiting South Africa + 5 International Travel Tips

Get The 10 Tips Here

http://www.antonswanepoelbooks.com/south_africa_5_facts.php

These 10 Tips can save you time, money, and make your trip go a lot smoother as well as help prevent lost luggage.

Anton Swanepoel

Made in the USA
San Bernardino, CA
14 March 2019